We Got Lost

Written by Trevor Kimball

Illustrated by Rowena King

Short *a* (CVC words)	Long *a* (VCe words)	Consonant *Gg* /g/	Consonant *Qq* /kw/
grab	cave	get	quick
lamp	plates	go	quit
last	safe	grab	
map	same	legs	
	take		

High-Frequency Words

all	our	walk
eat	soon	want
look	they	where

1

We take a walk.

They all look the same.
We get lost.

We want to eat soon.
We are wet.

We step in a cave.
We do not see where to go.

We find a lamp.
We find a map.

Quick!
We walk fast.
Our legs do not quit.

We are safe at last.
We grab plates.
We eat it up.